A POCKETFUL OF
P O E M S
AUSSIE FLAVOURED RHYMING VERSE

www.wilkinsonpublishing.com.au

Published by:
Wilkinson Publishing Pty Ltd
ACN 006 042 173
Level 4, 2 Collins St Melbourne, Victoria, Australia 3000
Ph: +61 3 9654 5446
www.wilkinsonpublishing.com.au

Cover art Lee Walker.
Internal design Lee Walker.

A catalogue record for this
book is available from the
National Library of Australia

Planned date of publication: October 2020
Title: A Pocketful of Poems
ISBN(s): 9781925927467 Printed – Paperback.
Printed and bound in Australia by Griffin, a part of Ovato

A POCKETFUL OF
POEMS

AUSSIE FLAVOURED RHYMING VERSE

MURRAY HARTIN

FOREWORD

I have said many times that Murray Hartin is Australia's modern-day Banjo Paterson.

Murray Hartin is a poet, first and foremost.

But from any perspective, and especially from the perspective of schoolchildren, he is a social commentator and a chronicler.

From an educational point of view, young people live in difficult times. Of course, they have the benefit of all the fandango technology, and they can use it. But without a facility with language and without an appreciation of literature, we are all diminished.

The stories that Murray Hartin tells are illustrative, often amusing, unapologetically blunt, but quintessentially Australian.

Thankfully, Murray is able to give poetry relevance, interest and beautiful rhythms. As he says in his introduction, 'Songs are just poetry with music and chorus'.

But at a time when young Australians want to know and want to learn, want to be involved and want to be excited by our history, I sense that they are being betrayed.

We have just emerged from awful experiences of drought and bushfire. Early on in this collection, Murray Hartin uses the rhythm of language and the euphony of rhyme to tell the story of drought with which too many Australians are unfamiliar.

In the poem Rain from Nowhere, the farmer, like many today, through circumstances beyond his control, feels a failure and 'there is no place in life for failure, he'd end it all tonight'.

Murray then shares with us the reality of family life in the bush. The farmer would prepare to 'blow away the blues'. But when he checked the 'roadside mailbox' he 'found a letter from his Dad'.

Kids, school kids, often think their dad does not understand.

No piece of modern history better captures the tragedy and triumphs of the bush in drought. Murray Hartin is their literary spokesman.

But just when you immerse yourself in the emotion of poetry like this, a new emotion is given expression by the same poet.

We then laugh at the typical bushie experience, the farmer having his first ride in a plane, 'Turbulence'.

It is immensely disturbing that in too many classrooms today, poetry is seen as 'too difficult'.

Yet poetry, well taught, can inspire, inform and foster a better understanding of our place in the world.

This anthology is essential reading Enjoyment is guaranteed. The pleasure that Murray Hartin has given to thousands and thousands of people, as he travels the bush, sharing his stories in verse – that pleasure, through this anthology, is available to every schoolchild in Australia.

For that, they should feel privileged.

It's now up to our teachers and the system. I urge you not to let the children down.

And Murray Hartin, stand tall. You have made, here, in verse, an indelible contribution to a better understanding of this beautiful but sometimes wilful country.

Alan Jones

INTRODUCTION

I love rhyming poetry.

Some people don't like it and yet they really love songs.

Well, songs are just poetry with music and a chorus.

Rap is rhyming poetry.

Hip Hop is rhyming poetry.

It's all beat-per-syllable delivery so you can rap out Banjo Paterson's famous poem The Man From Snowy River if you want.

It might take about 10 minutes because it's a long poem but you can certainly present it in rap-style.

Rhyme plays a huge role in our lives from the moment we're born.

Parents sing lullabies to their babies.

As kids we learn nursery rhymes.

We then read Dr Seuss and Roald Dahl and other children's authors.

Things are easier to learn if they rhyme.

That's why we remember lullabies and nursery rhymes.

That's why years later we can remember poems and songs.

Some of Australia's best modern-day poets are rock bands/country singers/rappers/hip hop artists.

Hilltop Hoods, Paul Kelly, Tones and I,
Archie Roach, 360, The Waifs, Iggy Azalea,
John Williamson –
they're all poets who have added music and
melody to their words.

When I was in Year 5 at Moree Public School
in 1973, my teacher, Mr Lawler, would make
us write poetry.

I loved it.

Fourteen years later in 1987, just before my
24th birthday, I stumbled across a poetry
competition at The Tamworth Country Music
Festival and, much to the surprise of myself
and my mates, I somehow won the final.

It changed my life.

Took me in a whole new direction.

The competition win led to a job as a
journalist with the local Tamworth
newspaper and in 1996 I decided to have a
crack at writing and reciting poems for
a living.

And I'm still doing it today.

I perform all across Australia at festivals,
corporate functions, sporting lunches
and charity dinners – lots and lots of
different venues.

I write yarns about my mates, serious poems,
nonsense poems and topical.

Writing poems, prose or short stories can be
a lot of fun.

It can also be therapeutic.

Converting what's in your head – your thoughts, your dreams, your aspirations, your problems, funny things that have happened – converting them to the written form can take a load off your mind and make you feel pretty good about yourself.

It's a bit of a buzz.

It doesn't have to be brilliant but, like anything, the more you do it, the more you practice, the better you'll become.

You don't have to share what you've written but you can if you choose.

It's up to you.

In the year 2000 my poem *Turbulence* made it to No. 16 on the National Country Music charts.

Rain From Nowhere has been printed in metropolitan newspapers and magazines across the country.

I wrote *The Ballad of Kev Koala and Ringtail Pete* on the morning of that competition final back in 1987.

They're all in this book – along with a selection of my other favourites.

I hope you like them.

And I hope they inspire you to write a few of your own.

Cheers.
Muz

CONTENTS

Spirit 1

Fishin' For Cod 5

Rain From Nowhere 10

Turbulence 15

The Slouch Hat 21

Big Jack 24

The Ballad of Kev Koala &
Ringtail Pete 27

The Farmer – The Pearl of Them All ... 29

The Quality of Life 32

Faster, Higher, Stronger 34

The Shopping Bags Fiasco 37

The Boys From Bungituppem 41

A Second Glance 44

The Canola Crops Near Cowra 46

Don't Go There 48

The Best Bloke I Know 49

Old Friends 51

Fishing With Fulvio 52

Colours 58

The Strength Within 61

Mrs Johnston's Chooks 63

A Pig's Lament 69

The Froggywogs, The Logs and
The Wagga Wagga Fog 70

Through The Eyes Of Banjo 72

Going back to school 74

SPIRIT

There's a beat beneath the Olgas,
Out there near Uluru,
Spreading south right to the Bight
And north to Kakadu.

Radiating to the shoreline
There's a pulse from east to west,
It defies true definition,
This strange feeling in your chest.

It's the Spirit of The Dreamtime,
It's the sweat of pioneers,
It's the Rainbow Serpent's teachings
Of more than 40,000 years.

It's the clash of many cultures,
The recipe's unique,
Reflected in our actions,
What we do and how we speak.

It's the scent of eucalyptus,
It's lamb chops on the barbie,
It's ANZAC Day and two-up
Down the pub with Uncle Harvey.

It's a nice fresh batch of lamingtons,
Whatever takes your fancy,
The everlasting stars
That lit up the night for Clancy.

It's the right to have opinions,
All open for debate,
It's the foreign-looking kid
Asking 'Owyagoin' Mate?'

It's the footy, it's the cricket,
It's every type of sport,
On the oval, in the water
Or the backyard tennis court.

It's the Royal Flying Doctor,
It's names like Cobb & Co,
A pie with sauce, an ice-cold beer,
The farm, the surf, the snow.

It's billy tea and damper
By a fire of gidgee coal,
A sunrise champagne breakfast
Where the colours touch your soul

Like a Namatjira painting,
That takes your breath away,
It's little bits of speech
Like 'okey dokey' and 'g'day'.

We spread the word in far-off countries
But the thrill you get for free
Is when you touch down on the tarmac
In our land that's girt by sea.

Sure we sing that daggy line
When we stand up with the crowd
In a sea of Green and Gold
'cause we're Aussies and we're proud.

It doesn't matter what you're wearing
When you're belting out that song,
Designer suits or riding boots
Or double-plugger thongs.

Just sing the words with passion
Perhaps a little bit off key
And you'll know The Land Down Under
Is the only place to be.

Beneath The Southern Cross,
It's fair dinkum and True Blue,

A Golden sprig of wattle,
The Boxing Kangaroo

It's Slouch Hats and Akubras,
It's the sweat-stained Baggy Green,
It's Hard Knocks Schools and PhDs
And all things in between.

It's a great big bunch of clichés
That sometimes hide the fact
When there's hard work to be done
We hook in and have a crack.

We unite in times of tragedy,
Fire, drought or flood,
Drop the tools and join the fight,
Maybe spill a bit of blood

For a neighbour, for a stranger,
For a battler, for a mate.
That's the Spirit of Australia,
That's what makes this country great.

So protect her and respect her
In all you say and do,
Be proud you are Australian
And make sure she's proud of you.

FISHIN' FOR COD

Killer, Quenten and Bloody Mick went
fishin' out west for cod,
They took Reschy along as their spiritual
guide, he was known as the Jamtin God.

The trek had been planned for six
long months and all was now in order,
They were ready to go to The Great Beyond,
just north of the Queensland border.

With a thousand yabbies, six hundred carp
and a mile or more of worms
They had the bait to lure the fish and meet
'em on equal terms.
For the cod that come from The Great
Beyond, near the Never Go Dry Lagoon,
Are the hardest cod in the world to catch,
they don't waltz to the fishermen's tune.

Well, the four-wheel-drive was sardine-
packed, the trailer stacked ten foot high
With boats and tackle and food and grog
the boys weren't gonna go dry.

They got to the river at the crack of dawn,
an eerie mist on the water,
The Jamtin God stood up and proclaimed
'Bringeth the lambs to the slaughter'.
They set their lines, they made their camp
then Killer opened a beer,
He drank a toast to a healthy catch and
said *'Tell the cod we're here'*.
A tinkering bell was the first alert that the
fish were on the bite
But the line hit the water, springer and all,
and vanished out of sight.

Ten more went as a frenzy began, there was
little the boys could do,
There was just no chance of grabbin' the
lines or their hands'd be cut in two.
The rot went on for three long days, the
party was spent to a man
Except, of course, for The Jamtin God, who
had one final plan.

So they hooked the carcass of a flyblown
ewe to the anchor from one of the boats,
The sheep had been dead for a good two
weeks and stank like a thousand goats.

They secured the lot with a length of chain
to an old rusty plough by a tree,
Said The Jamtin God *'If the cod breaks that
he's far too good for me!'*
Well, they whistled their way to their
sleeping bags, 'twas a jovial fishermen's choir
Then Quenten sang some Al Jolson songs by
the flickering light of the fire.
They drifted off to the Land of Nod ... but
soon awoke in fright
As the murderous sound of a fish-drawn
plough came thundering through the night!

The plough was headed straight for the
camp, the chain was glowing red,
Gum trees snapped like matchsticks and the
boys thought they were dead
But Bloody Mick, he cracked the whip and
said *'Quick, get in the truck!*
*'We can catch this sucker with half a chance
... and given an ounce of luck.'*
So they followed the plough for an hour or
so 'til the fish had finished its run
Then they tied the chain to the four-wheel
drive and the battle had begun.

Killer jumped in the driver's seat and with a
look of satisfaction
Said *'The bloody cod's as good as caught, get
ready for some action!'*
The engine roared, the tyres spun, the boys
were pushing hard,
The sun came up ... and the sun went down
and they'd gone forward just a yard.
But they inched ahead, the cod was beat,
the boys let out a cheer
As this Moby Dick of the Inland Sea he
started to appear.

With a mouth as big as a block of flats,
there was nothin' he couldn't swolla,
He was forty foot from lip to gill ... with
plenty more to folla!
Now, Killer was clockin' up overtime, the
tyres were all but bald
While the others watched as the fish came
out ... and the river began to fall!
And all across the countryside the rivers
were running dry,
From Mungindi to Shepparton the folk
were asking *'Why?'*

The Darling was barely a trickle, the
Murray ran hardly a drop
'Til the PM flew in from Canberra and he
begged the boys to stop.

See drought had hit the country bad and
they'd finally found the cause
So the boys cut loose that Super Cod to
national applause!
The river levels rose again, the
tragedy averted,
The fishing party headed home a
trifle disconcerted.

Now, they'll tell you they've captured
some big cod since
But the biggest without a doubt
Was the monster they caught but had
to release
To save the land from drought!

RAIN FROM NOWHERE

His cattle didn't get a bid, mind you they
were fairly bloody poor,
What was he going to do? He couldn't feed
them anymore,
The dams were all but dry, hay was thirteen
bucks a bale
And last month's talk of rain was just a
fairytale,
His credit had run out, no chance to pay
what's owed,
Bad thoughts ran through his head as he
drove down Gully Road.

'Geez, great-Grandad bought the place back
in 1898,
'Now I'm such a useless bastard, I'll have to
shut the gate.
'I can't feed my wife and kids, not like Dad
and those before,
'Crikey, Grandma kept it going while Pop
fought in the war.'
With depression now his master, he
abandoned what was right,
There's no place in life for failure, he'd end
it all tonight.

10

There were still some things to do, he'd
have to shoot the cattle first,
Of all the jobs he'd ever done, that would
be the worst.
Then he'd shower, watch the news, they'd
all sit down for tea,
Read his kids a bedtime story, watch some
more TV,
Kiss his wife goodnight, say he was off to
shoot some roos
Then in a paddock far away he'd blow
away the blues.
But he drove in the gate and stopped, as he
always had,
To check the roadside mailbox and found a
letter from his Dad.
Now his Dad was not a writer, Mum did all
the cards and mail
But he knew the writing from the
notebooks that he'd kept from cattle sales.
He sensed the nature of its contents, felt
the moisture in his eyes,
Just the fact his Dad had written was
enough to make him cry.

'Son, I know it's bloody tough, it's a cruel
and twisted game,
'This life upon the land when you're
screaming out for rain,
'There's no candle in the darkness, not a
single speck of light
'But mate, don't let the demon get you, you
have to do what's right,
'I don't know what's in your head but push
the nasty thoughts away
'See, you'll always have your family at the
back end of the day.'

'You have to talk to someone, and yeah, I
know I rarely did
'But you have to think about Fiona and think
about the kids.
'I'm worried about you son, you haven't
phoned for quite a while
'And I know the road you're on 'cause I've
walked every bloody mile.
'The date? December 7 back in 1983,
'Behind the shed I had the shotgun rested in
the brigalow tree.

12

'See, I'd borrowed way too much to buy the
Johnson place
'Then it didn't rain for years and we got
bombed by interest rates,
'The bank was at the door, I didn't think I
had a choice,
'I began to squeeze the trigger ... and that's
when I heard your voice.
'You said "Where are you, Daddy? It's time
to play our game"
"'I've got Squatter all set up, we might get
General Rain."'
'It really was that close and you're the one
that stopped me, son
'And you're the one that taught me there's no
answer in a gun.
'Just remember people love you, good mates
won't let you down
'And look, you might have to swallow pride
and take that job in town,
'Just 'til things come good, son, you've always
got a choice
'And when you get this letter ring me 'cause
I'd love to hear your voice.'

Well he cried and laughed and shook his
head and put the truck in gear,
Shut his eyes and hugged his Dad in a
vision that was clear,
Dropped the cattle at the yards, put the
truck away,
Filled the troughs the best he could and fed
his last ten bales of hay.
Then he strode towards the homestead,
shoulders back, head held high,
He still knew the road was tough but there
was purpose in his eye.
He called his wife and children, who'd lived
through all his pain,
Hugs said more than words – he'd come
back to them again,
Then they talked of silver linings, how
good times always follow bad,
Then he walked towards the phone, picked
it up and rang his Dad.
And while the kids set up the Squatter, he
hugged his wife again,
Then they heard the roll of thunder and
they smelt the smell of rain.

TURBULENCE

Here's a tale of Billy Hayes from out near
Alice Springs,
A wild young ringer who in his day had done
some crazy things.
He'd jumped bulls over fences, raced a colt
up Ayers Rock,
See, his legs weren't built for walking, they
were made for riding stock.
A legend 'round the rodeos from Aileron
to Broome,
An untried horse at 6am was saddle-broke
by noon.
No form of equine foolery Bill wasn't game
to try,
Only one thing ever spooked him – he was
way too scared to fly.
*'Ay, if I was meant to do it I'd have feathers
and a beak,*
*'You take the plane there in a day. I'll drive
and waste a week.*
*'I've been told they're safe as houses and
mechanically they're sound,*
*'I don't see no rope or bridle so, ay, I'm
sticking on the ground!'*

But one day Billy got a phone call from his
mate in Adelaide
Who'd got his girl in trouble so the wedding
cards were played.
*'Aw, Bill, I don't care how ya do it, ya can beg
or steal or borra,*
'But mate you've gotta take the plane, ay,
'cause the big day's on tomorra!'
Well, Billy cursed and spat it, said *'That
dopey bloody coot,'*
*'He knows I'd jump on anything that's
comin' out a chute.*
*'I've caught stallions that'd kill ya, caught
bulls gone off their brain,*
*'Never thought there'd come the day I'd hafta
catch a plane!'*
He legged it to the airport, he thought
'Well this is it'.
The lady at the counter asked *'Where would
you like to sit?'*
He said *'Ahh, you know that black box thing
they always seem to find,*
*'Well you can stick me right inside it if ya
wouldn't bloody mind!'*

The lady smiled politely and said *'Sir, I'll just take your bag'*.

He said *'I don't bloody think so and by the way it's called a swag'*.

Bill was sweating buckets when they finally cleared the strip,

He had his seatbelt on that tight he was bleeding from the hip

But when they levelled out he stopped shaking at the knees,

Looked around, relaxed and thought *'This flyin' game's a breeze'*.

He clipped his belt undone, stretched out in his seat,

Well, he couldn't stretch that far because his swag was at his feet.

Then the captain crackled something, Bill asked a hostess what was said,

'Sir, you'd better buckle up there's some turbulence ahead'.

He said 'Turbulence, what's that?' *'Sir it's pockets caused by heat*

'And when it gets severe it can throw you from your seat.'

He said *'Throw me, I'll be buggered'*, he
pushed his seat right back,
Wrapped his legs around his swag and
stuck his left hand through the strap,
He jammed down his Akubra, he was ready
now to ride
Then things got pretty bumpy and Billy
yelled *'OUTSIDE!'*
The plane she dropped a thousand feet,
rose up five hundred more,
When his head near hit the ceiling he gave
a mighty roar,
*'I've rode all through the Territ'ry and never
come unstuck,*
*'So give me all you've got big bird and buck
you bastard buck!'*
And while the passengers were screaming
in fear of certain death
Billy whooped and hollered 'til he near ran
out of breath.
You would've thought that canvas swag
was welded to his ass
And before the ringer knew it he'd bucked
up to business class!

There seemed no way to tame this creature, it had ten gears and reverse,

That didn't worry Billy, he just bucked on through to first!

He'd done somersaults with twists on this mongrel mount from hell,

He yelled out to the pilot *'For Christ's sake, ring the bell!'*

Poor old Bill was bleeding from the bugle, he had cuts above both eyes,

If you weren't there on the spot you prob'ly think I'm telling lies.

He'd been upside down, inside out, done flips and triple spins,

You might've seen some great rides in your time but hands down Billy wins.

The flight returned to normal, Bill was flat out on the deck,

Still stuck to his swag but geez, he looked a bloody wreck.

He pulled himself together, stood up and raised his hat,

He said *'I've had some tough trips in my time but never one like that.*

*'An eight-second spin in Alice proves you're
made of sturdy stuff,*
*'I was on there near a minute and I reckon
that's enough.'*
Well the first class folk were dumbstruck at
this crazy ringer's feat
But Bill just grabbed a Crownie and he
walked back to his seat.
Now years have passed and Bill's long give
the bucking game away,
Too many breaks and dusty miles for far
too little pay,
Now planes are not a problem, in fact he'd
rather fly than ride
And when you talk about his maiden
voyage his chest puffs out with pride.
*'You can talk about your Rocky Neds and
that old Chainsaw bloke,*
*'I'd ride 'em both without a rope and roll a
bloody smoke.*
*'There's cowboys 'round who think they're
hot, well they ain't tasted heat*
*''Til they've ridden time on Turbulence at
30,000 feet!'*

THE SLOUCH HAT

There's a Slouch Hat in my lounge-room,

Pristine and never worn,

Standing watch atop a globe

Dawn til dusk and dusk til dawn,

It will never go to battle,

Never ask the question 'Why?'

But it sings to me A Sappers Lullaby.

It won't play footy by The Pyramids,

Won't taste Kokoda's mud,

Won't feel the heat of Vietnam,

Won't be stained by good men's blood,

It won't trade shrapnel in the chaos

On a beach at ANZAC Cove

But it tells me quietly why the rough men go,

Men like my mate Coops,

Who gave the hat to me,

Who back the Engineers

As they clear the IEDs,

Thirty feet apart,
Treading softly, staggered file,
Under the Afghan sun they walk the
danger miles.

And I've shared beers and laughs
with Timmy
And I've looked him in the eye,
Heard him talk about lost mates
And I've seen a tough man cry,
Just like those who've gone before him –
And they may go on forever –
And the slouch hat, well, it binds them
all together.

With just a sideways glance
It can set my brain to work,
Recall the deeds of Albert Jacka,
Hear the pledge of Ataturk,
Eric Bogle sings Waltzing Matilda
And the lyrics haunt my mind
As I think of all the heroes left behind.

But the Rising Sun will not forget them
As it shines on new recruits,
Brave young men and women
Bold as brass in shiny boots,
Duntroon and Kapooka,
Passing every test
And beneath the Slouch Hat's brim they'll
do their best.

So that Slouch Hat in my lounge room
It won't travel overseas
But it takes me on great journeys,
Reminds me why I'm free,
A symbol of Australia,
No surrender, few regrets
And a shrine to those now gone, Lest
We Forget.

BIG JACK

Jack Baldock, now he was a legend
Whose top days had long disappeared
But to the people out west he was one
of the best
A man respected and feared.

A drover who knew all the stock routes,
He'd spent most of his days working cattle
But with the outbreak of war he answered
the call
And courageously charged into battle.

He went over the top at Gallipoli
For his orders commanded him so
But as his mates fell like flies he learnt
to despise
The generals who butchered the show.

He won no Victoria Crosses
'Though it was said that he'd earned his
fair share
For his comrades all knew in the thick
of a blue
Big Jack would always be there.
When the ANZACs were told to withdraw
Jack said *'It's about flamin' time.*
'The British were wrong, the death list too long,
'The top brass committed a crime.'

Now when he went back to Australia
He went home to the Kimberley Ranges,
To the Derby Hotel where they remember
so well
Of when Jack had to sort out some strangers.

These drongos had cruised in
from Broome,
They were solid and brainless and mean,
They went flamin' wild, scaring
women and child
'Til Big Jack arrived on the scene.

Well, Jack told the boys to get packin'
And silence fell over the street,
'Though outgunned five to one when Big
Jack was done
He was the only one left on his feet.

And the time at the Derby rodeo
On a strange horse 'cause his had gone lame,
On this thing called The Noggin he won the
ropin' and doggin',
Yeah Jack was the best in the game.

But these days were now long behind him,
I sat as he lay in his bed,
I still can remember that day in December
And the last parting words that he said.

'If by deed or by luck you find glory
'Don't be makin' a fuss or big noise
'For no matter what strikes ya or how many
folk like ya
'To your mates you're just one of the boys.'

'Just do what you think is the right thing
'And if you're wrong own up to your sins
'For you're not worth a cracker or a tin
of tobacco
'If you don't cop your knocks on the chin.'

Jack's once strong voice it grew weaker,
He knew the end of his life it was near
And with one final breath accepted
his death,
No regrets … no anger … no fear.

THE BALLAD OF KEV KOALA & RINGTAIL PETE

Kev Koala rode into town
A gun slung from each hip,
He was the meanest son of a bear
Ever to suck on a eucalypt.
And the reason he travelled through dust
and heat
Was to challenge the gun of Ringtail Pete.

Now Kev was a bear who was quick with a
gun
And was chasing a reputation,
And his young mind reasoned the quickest
way there
Was to knock off the best in the nation.
So with adrenaline pumping at a
furious rate
He prepared for the fight that would
determine his fate.

Ringtail Pete, as you may well know,
Was a possum of evil persuasion,
Of equal ability with pistol or fists
When involved in an altercation
And many a man was no longer alive
Due to lightning speed of his Colt 45.
Kev found Pete at the Marsupial Bar
At the Wheelabarraback Saloon,

The possum played poker with his
roughneck mates
As the town clock struck high noon,
So the scene was set for an epic showdown
That would liven the streets of the small
outback town.

Kev said *'Ringtail Pete, I call you outside*
'To challenge the speed of your gun.
'And I'll bask in the title of best in the land
'Which must surely be mine when I've won.'
The possum said *'Kid, I've faced your kind*
in the past,
'You're only a boy so pray that you're fast.'

The possum stood up from the table
And scratched the back of his head,
'You'd better say what you wanna say
now, boy
''Cause it's hard to talk when you're dead.'
There they stood face to face, ready to go,
One was a kid and one was a pro.

They buried poor Kevin the following day
And Ringtail Pete attended
To say a few words at the grave of the boy
Whose soul towards heaven ascended.
'The kid shoulda learnt that out here in
the west,
'When your life is a gun, make sure you're
the best.'

THE FARMER – THE PEARL OF THEM ALL

Australia is chock-full of champions
And history will keep safe their names,
We share moments of proud men
and women
Who have climbed to the top of their game,
They provide us with great inspiration
But if I may make a very big call,
If the aim is to recognise champions
I think The Farmer's the Pearl of Them All.

See the tough game he's in never ends
And the playing field's often quite rough,
You need wet stuff to fill up the rain gauge,
Talent and hope aren't enough.
Resilience plays a huge factor,
Without it the greatest may fall
And our champion has got it in spades,
The Farmer, The Pearl of Them All.

Plus courage to push through the
hard times,
You need it to last on the land,
While the Rain Gods can smile on
you sweetly
Control can still slip from your hands.

Too much is as bad as too little,
A flood rocks him right to the core
But he mops up and continues the battle,
The Farmer, The Pearl of Them All.

Sometimes there are knee-jerk reactions
From those who are desperate for votes
Who pretend to be well-versed in matters
But wouldn't know chick peas from oats.
While he tries to make sense of
this madness
That again puts his back to the wall,
Each day he heads out to the paddock,
The Farmer, The Pearl of Them All.

Look, it's not all bad luck and
crook seasons,
When the planets align life is sweet.
He knows when he gets a fair go
His produce is real hard to beat,
He'll knock the froth off a couple of
cold ones
And most likely have a few more
To celebrate the life he has chosen
The Farmer – The Pearl of Them All.

So next time the talk turns to heroes,
A subject of much great debate
And you discuss who befits such a title,
Spare a thought for our battling mate.
In the history of all things Australian
He has well-earned the right to walk tall
So please raise a glass to our champion
The Farmer – The Pearl of Them All.

Inspired by Will Ogilvie's classic poem
The Pearl of Them All.

THE QUALITY OF LIFE

Written for the kids at Camp Quality.

Life is what you make it,
That's if you're free to make a choice,
Some roar loudly at the challenge,
Others struggle for a voice.

If you're blessed with opportunity
It becomes a simple game,
When things turn sour, don't look elsewhere
You've only got yourself to blame.

Don't deny your failure,
Extract wisdom from the fall,
For if you examine those around you
You'll find your life's not rough at all.

There's a special group of children
Whose time on earth is brief,
The pain and hardship they endure
Is way beyond belief.

See cancer's not a word to them,
It's a sentence they accept
And while the clock is running down
They'll make the most of what is left.

These kids don't crave your pity
They just wanna have some fun,
Get together with their mates
And swim and fly and run.

What value on a laughing face?
What price upon a grin?
From these youngsters who are in a game
They know they cannot win.

But that won't break their spirit,
Quit's a word they can't pronounce,
Their time for living can't be changed
So it's the quality that counts.

Find inspiration in their courage,
Help them dance that final mile,
The reward is rich yet simple,
The smile of a child.

FASTER, HIGHER, STRONGER

The dreams of children know

no boundaries,

Imagination is their realm,

Destination undecided

They cheer loudly from the helm.

Pushing through uncharted waters,

Vanquished demons in their wake,

Superheroes of a journey

Only they can undertake.

But reality looms large,

A sober world dismisses fools

But dreamtime's true disciples

Don't bow down to sober rules.

Youthful confidence makes statements,

Disbelievers draw their swords

But when commitment teams

with passion

Youthful dreams won't be ignored.

'Faster, Higher, Stronger'

Is the creed that fuels their soul,

Striving for that invitation

That in itself is pure gold.

The lure of standing tall

On history's greatest stage

Consigns sacrifice and heartache

To a full stop on a page.

Chase the black line, chase the white line,

Chase the clock to chase the dream,

Your limit is your target

And there's nothing in between.

It's a test of who you are,

No one else can make that play,

What you're destined for tomorrow

Depends on what you do today.

It's not for adulation

Nor beating of the chest,

It's the pride in competition

And to simply do your best

But if the Southern Cross starts dancing
To Advance Australia Fair
And you're standing on the dais
It's a time for all to share.
Don't fight the tears of raw emotion,
Open up and let them flow,
Breathe in that special moment
That few will ever know,
Sing out loud and pound your heart,
A proud member of the team
And don't let it be forgotten
It all started as a dream.

THE SHOPPING BAGS FIASCO

It's a finite world we live in,
Of that there's little doubt,
The ice caps and the ozone
And the trees are running out.

I recycle when I can
But I'm being driven mad
By those environmental 'Save the Planet'
BRIGHT GREEN SHOPPING BAGS!

Don't pretend you haven't bought 'em,
They bloody got me too,
The voice of guilt booms through the aisles
When you're trying to buy some food.

A constant message warns you
'Plastic kills' and *'It's your choice'*,
So you buy the bright green
shopping bags
Just to stop the voice.

But now the herbal groovy checkout chick
Who used to snarl and look away
Fills your new bags with a smile
And says *'Have a lovely day'*.

And the new bags hold much more
So it's not just conservation,
Plus they're easy on the grip
And don't cut your circulation.
So, on the journey to your car,
The usual half a mile,
You think the bags are pretty cool
And you crack a little smile.

You get home feeling fairly smug,
Pack the food away,
Stick the new bags in the cupboard
And that's where they bloody stay!
You never take them to the shops!
You don't remember 'til you're there!
So you're back to using plastic
And the checkout chick just glares.

So you buy more bright green
shopping bags
To get her back on side
And they end up in the cupboard
Where the other mongrels died!

Well, they're not dead, they're just asleep,
I mean nitro glycerin
Couldn't kill these bags,
They're made of poly-propylene.
Environmentally friendly?!
They'd survive a nuclear blast,
We're talking heavy-duty gear
That makes plastic look like grass.

So you stick some in your car,
You won't forget them now,
Well of course you bloody do,
You just can't work out how.
It doesn't matter where you put them,
In the boot or in the front,
You could hang 'em 'round your neck,
You'll still only use them once!

They keep selling me these bags
And they know I've got a stack,
In the car, in the cupboard
And don't forget the granny flat.
I want to do the right thing
So I keep on buying more
Just because I forget
To bring the ones I bought before.

Meanwhile, the price of poly-propylene
Is going through the roof,
Well, I don't know that for sure,
I haven't got much proof

But someone's making money
And it sure as hell ain't me,
I've got a thousand bright green
shopping bags
And they cost three bucks a piece!

So while I'd love to save the planet,
And the green bags are fantastic,
My accountant said, to save my house,
I have to stick to plastic.

THE BOYS FROM BUNGITUPPEM

The Wyjacummear Oval was green and
freshly mowed
For a challenge had been issued to the mob
from down the road
By the Wyjacummear Rugby team who
thought 'emselves good things
To towel their neighbours up and be
crowned as rugby kings.
Now the boys from Bungituppem were a
pretty handy side,
The club was full of history and the
players full of pride
So they went to Wyjacummear full
of anticipation,
Searching for a win to enhance
their reputation.
Bungituppem won the toss, the match
was underway
But their captain, Walter Wombat, was
taken out of play.

A vicious brawl erupted but the ref
controlled the tiff
And said the match would be abandoned if
they didn't stop the biff.
Both teams settled down from the initial
mad melee
And soon the crowd was mesmerised by
some scintillating play
But every great attacking move was met
by strong defence
And at halftime the outcome still was
anybody's guess.
Wyjacummear came out firing after a rev
up at the break
And with a 40-metre field goal Phil the Fox
made no mistake.
Three points up and with the wind they
took on a 10-man game
But Bungituppem kept on comin' and
refused to do the same.
They ran the ball from everywhere –
lineout, scrum and maul,
With not much time to go they made one
last desperate call.

Walter Wombat, playing pivot, looked to
run it wide
But with a clever little flick pass picked up
Willy Wagtail back inside.
The Wagtail went through the gap, the
bird looked set to score
But he was met by Eddie Emu who took
him ball-'n'-all.
Bungituppem won the second phase with a
solid forward drive,
Seconds on the clock, the ball was still alive!
It came back to the Wombat who was full
of many tricks,
He sidestepped through, beat Phil the Fox
and scored beneath the sticks.
He took his time with the conversion and
as the final whistle blew
Came in round-the-corner style and put the
ball straight through.
The Wyjacummear boys were shattered, as
was their rugby dream,
While Walter Wombat was quick to praise
the efforts of his team
But it was he who proved the difference,
which was best summed up by Macca,
Speaking of the Wombat's sidestep said *'It
really is a cracker'*.

A SECOND GLANCE

A second glance, a look away,
A face that scorns the light of day
Stares right back and mumbles words,
Incoherent, rarely heard.
The well-dressed stranger moves along,
Briefly thinks of what went wrong
Then, like all the other grains of salt,
(Not my problem, not my fault)
The homeless figure disappears
Just as he's done for months — for years.

But look beyond the bottle brown
That helps to wash the anger down,
Matted beard, tormented eyes,
This is where the story lies.
A wife, a child, future bright,
Drunk driver on a rainy night
Stole it all, he couldn't cope,
Failed bids with pills and rope
Saw him drift into the park
Where kindred souls move through
the dark.
The bottle helps absorb the blows
From memories that won't let go

And while they lodge a guilty plea
The price he pays is sanity.
So much more than just a homeless man,
Do passers-by dare understand
Or take a journey in those shoes,
Lose everything there is to lose,
Asking God for reasons why,
Easier to walk on by.

Each day the tragedies unfold,
The stories though are rarely told,
A thousand pages on the street,
Heroes you may never meet,
Different paths, same result,
Just another grain of salt.

But those who search behind the mask
And choose to undertake the task
To offer light to darkened minds,
Ensuring no one's left behind,
Walk through a door that few can see,
And fewer still can find the key,
To thoughts and dreams long cast aside
By those who thought the love had died
But resurrected by the quote
Of just three words – *'there's always hope'*.

CANOLA CROPS NEAR COWRA

Nature's colours can't be captured in
their purity and glow,
It's a thought that tortures artists, as
only artists know,
While the scene is rich and vivid in a
rich and fertile mind
On the journey to the canvas something
special's left behind
But I'll share with you a vision that will
never go away,
The canola crops near Cowra on a warm
September day.

We headed out from Canberra for south-
west New South Wales
With the old colt, Billy Rowlands,
fertilising bushman's tales
And he's got a way of speaking the
country folk know well,
*'Colt, six weeks ago out here the place was
dry as hell*
*'But then we got the rain like I thought we
bloody would*
*'And colt, there's canola crops out here that are
prettybloody good.'*

As I absorbed the Old Colt's character the
miles quickly passed,
Laughter silenced silence and each yarn
was his last,
The scent of spring was heavy on a fresh
and gentle breeze
That gave away its presence as it danced its
way through trees,
Then came forth the vision that took my
breath away,
The canola crops near Cowra on a warm
September day.

Like a dangerous hue of gold that alters
minds and fathers' dreams
It was oozing over fence lines, paddocks
bursting at the seams,
A patchwork-quilted countryside
hypnotising passers-by,
A sun-kissed magic melody composed by
earth and sky,
And as I go through life I'll remember all
the way
The canola crops near Cowra on a warm
September day.

DON'T GO THERE

I heard a whisper from the crisper, fair
dinkum, ridgy didge,
You know, the place you keep your vegies
in the bottom of the fridge.
I hadn't looked in there for ages and I
wasn't gonna start,
The noise was getting louder, like the
pounding of my heart.

It could've been a mutant broccoli or a
carrot giving birth
Or some Triffid-like potato like you've
never seen on earth,
Or even worse, my flatmate's curry, geez,
my guts began to heave,
Here it was September and he cooked it
New Year's Eve!

I wasn't going near it, it was enough to
make you spew
So I packed my bags and left, it seemed the
only thing to do.
I wrote a note for Marty and I left it on
the gate,
It read *'Your dinner's in the crisper, I hope
you like it, mate.'*

THE BEST BLOKE
I KNOW

He's the best bloke I know, he's honest
and he's fair,
He's got the type of qualities that now
seem pretty rare,
He taught me right from wrong, taught
me how to give and share,
Now the only thing that's changed him
is the colour of his hair.

I've known him all my life, he's watched
me as I grew
And it's no secret round the traps that
we've had the odd good blue
But I've sometimes done it tough and
he's always helped me through,
I think the man's a champion and I
reckon you would too.

Yet there's nothing in the record books
to tell you what he's done,
He never shore two hundred and he
never made a ton

But he did his share of shearing and he
made his share of runs,
The bloke knows how to work and
knows how to have some fun.

And while his passion for the horses
hasn't done much for his wealth,
The man is rich on living and just glad
he's got his health,
He never would complain while there's
tucker on the shelf,
He'd give you what he's got and go
without himself.

Now his hair is snowy grey and his face
is leather-tanned,
He isn't rich, isn't famous but he does
the best he can,
You'll probably never meet him but it's
not hard to understand
The best bloke I know is Kevin Hartin,
my old man.

OLD FRIENDS

Although distance is divisive
And time can play its role
True friendship lasts forever,
Burning deep within the soul.
Memories, like magic,
Make the present fade away
And they give you rite of passage
To the world of yesterday
Where it only costs a smile
For a journey through the years
And the smile lingers still
When reality appears.
Those days are always with us
As the rest of life unfolds,
Adding fuel to the fire,
The fire in our soul.
But while memories are golden
Some things can't be replaced,
Your youth now walks towards you
In a warm and lived-in face.
The smile is contagious
The handshake lasts forever,
Time has to step aside
When old friends get together.

FISHING WITH FULVIO

I've spun some yarns, spread some bull and
told some monster tales
In regard to wild fishing trips and cod as
big as whales,
Each one has its merits, some might even
make you smile
But this next one is the best one that I've
heard in quite a while.
Not in terms of size of fish or huge
amounts of beer,
But the way it all panned out was on the
borderline of weird.
See Fulvio had all the gear when it came
to fishin'
And a weekend on the river was like a
three-month expedition.
He made Rex Hunt look underdone,
nothing left to chance,
He'd say *'When the music plays, my friends,
you must know how to dance'*.
Now Darkie just loved drinking and when
it came to fishing, mate,
Well, six-packs were his favourite catch,
he'd use his tongue for bait,
So in a small boat on the Gwydir out near
Crazy Lockhart's spread,

Well, the events that soon unfolded, you
know they're lucky they're not dead.
They had seven pounds of prawn heads in
a shrimp-net catching bait
But Fulvio's line was flaccid, no fish to fill
the plate.
He said *'Darkie, pull the anchor, we'll head a
bit upstream'*
Which snapped his snoozy sidekick from
another senseless dream.
Now downstream in a real deep hole there
lived a monster cod
And he somehow got a sniff of these
crustaceans sent from God.
He was drooling through his gills – it was
find this food or die,
He hadn't had a decent feed since that cow
drowned in July.
Now when it came to perfect timing,
Darkie took the prize,
The anchor reached the shrimp-net just as
the cod arrived.
It hit 'em both, took the lot, an explosive
burst of power
Then torpedoed down the Gwydir at a
hundred miles an hour.

It knocked the lock undone on the solar-
powered fridge
So Darkie cracked a can one-handed as
they passed the Pally Bridge.
Two locals overhead said *'Crikey, that things
got some grunt'*,
They couldn't see the dorsal fin fifteen feet
out front.
Yeah, this small electric motor that was flat
out beating eggs
Now had a turbo-cod injector and gee whiz
it had some legs.
They were bouncing off the banks as the
cod increased the pace,
He had a shrimp-net full of prawns and an
anchor in his face.
One thing he knew for sure, he wasn't
hanging for dessert
But the more he upped the speed, well, the
more it flamin' hurt.
The scene was just a blur as they came
'round Wattle Tops,
The cod, the boat, the boys on board – it
was like the Keystone Cops.
See there wasn't any noise, well, apart from
Darkie spewin',

From the bank, Sprat Broderick thought
'What are these boofheads doin'?'
He threw out one more cast,
understandably perplexed
And as Cod & Co went flying by you know
what happened next.
Sprat's favourite spinner hooked the boat,
there was little time to think,
He had to maintain his composure or go
headfirst in the drink.
He went sprinting for the water and with
the situation covered
Sprat was skiing down the Gwydir in a pair
of double pluggers
Behind a boat pulled by a cod, two freaked-
out mates on deck,
A ski jump fast approaching and a chance
to break his neck.
Someone lesser would've panicked but
Sprat was way too cool,
He summed up the situation and yelled
'Listen here, you fools,'
*'That's a cod you've got out front, throw out
more anchor chain,*
*'You need to play him for a while or he'll just
go off his brain!'*

55

Fulvio fed more chain but yelled a warning
back to Sprat,
*'There's a ski jump coming up, you'd better
keep your mind on that.'*
Yes, the Moree Ski Extravaganza was being
held there at the weir,
The jump event got started just as this
circus act appeared.
Sprat crossed the wake to build more
thrust then cut back right on time,
With rod in hand he hit the ramp — and fed
out a bit more line.
They say he cleared 300 feet, a record that
still stands,
But as he landed, thongs intact, things got
out of hand.
The cod ran out of river, he u-turned and
doubled back
Which whipped the boat onto the bank in a
stupefying stack.
Sprat raced up and grabbed his trophy
then the river turned to foam
As the cod spat out the anchor and geared
his fins for home.

Fulvio's fishing days are over, the
flashbacks make him scream,
Darkie's racing speedboats with the
NSW team,
Sprat's double-plugger thongs, well, they
coated them in bronze,
In the world of ski-jump heroes Sprat's
bigger than The Fonz
While out at Pally there's a monster cod
who once a week still gets the shivers
When Crazy Lockhart feasts on prawns
and throws the heads into the river.

COLOURS

What are the colours of Australia? Are
they simply green and gold
Or the grey that haunts a city in a winter
wet and cold?
Where the drizzle drowns the bitumen, its
blackness oozing pain
Before swirling down a gutter to find the
sea again.
A sea that harbours anger in a pounding
mid-year storm
And yet a sea that offers comfort when the
weather's clear and warm,
Where the whitecaps crown an ocean that
is every shade of blue,
Crashing to a golden shore, that's Australia
through and through.
See the bright zinc noses glisten beneath
hair as black as coal
Or the light blond locks of lifeguards on a
Bondi Beach patrol.
But has Australia more to offer than
merely surf and sand?
Well, the answer to the question lies within
the Rainbow Land.

For if you venture far away from the beach
and city streets
You might see the golden splendour of a
ripened field of wheat.
Or a fresh-ploughed North West paddock
on an apparent endless plain
Where the dark brown earth turns darker
when it's drenched by soothing rain
That sings songs upon a tin roof where,
underneath, a homestead wife
Is laughing with her children as they drink
the smell of life.
This brings a pearly smile to a sunburnt
farmer's face
And he gives thanks to the heavens for
another act of grace.
Or wander to a valley where the magic fruit
of vines
Is caressed by master makers 'til it fills a
glass with wine.
A rich burgundy or chardonnay, each a
colour in itself,
All destined for the darkness of a dusty
cellar shelf.
Keep on heading westward across this wide
brown land
And you'll marvel at The Simpson and its
shifting desert sands.

Sun-bleached brown and yellow as they
struggle to escape
To an horizon which by heat-waves has
been twisted out of shape.
Then push on to The Centre to see what it
holds for you
And you'll stare in sheer amazement at the
sight of Uluru.
The red-hot Rock at midday is a scene you
won't forget
Then you'll watch its colour change as the
sun begins to set.
Those harsh and vivid visions which by
day were burning bright
Take on softer, pastel hues as they usher in
the night.
For Nature is an artist and her canvas is
the Earth
And each day is a masterpiece transcending
mortal worth.
In her rich Australian gallery her paintings
have no peer,
From a jet-black moonless night to running
water, crystal-clear,
From a snow-capped Kosciuszko to a forest
charred by flame
Every worldly colour lies within Australia's
aqua frame.

THE STRENGTH WITHIN

Life's a constant battle,

How you think is how you cope,

You can submit to hardship meekly

Or you can grab it by the throat.

You can take the things that can't be done

And find a way they can,

It's what makes the girl a woman

And what makes the boy a man.

But the war is never over,

Some days are won while some are lost

But it's the fight that forges character

And the result is worth the cost,

For if you tap that inner strength

You can rise above the rest

And take pride in your achievements

When you know you've done your best.

But the true test is in your heart

And you'll discover who you are

When you've given it your all

And you somehow raise the bar.

When you find that extra second
That they told you can't be found,
When you crawl up off the canvas
To fight and win the final round.
It's never saying 'never',
It's 'I'll just do a couple more'
That takes you to that magic level
And opens up the champions' door.
So if there's one simple rule in life,
Well, perhaps then this is it,
The quitters never win
And the winners never quit.

MRS JOHNSTON'S CHOOKS

It was the harshest crime to have hit the
station's books,
Some dirty low-life scum had rustled Mrs
Johnston's chooks.
The robber bagged the best of them and
took the rest for luck,
Forty-seven leghorns, fifteen bantams and
a duck.

The pride of all the district was Mrs
Johnston's flock,
From her mighty leghorn roosters to her
little bantam cock.
'We'll have to put our best on this,' said
Senior Sergeant Kiley,
So the call went out, loud and clear, for
Stock Detective Riley.

A slow-talkin' sort of casual bloke but
ruthless just the same,
He was known to all as 'Roundup' and
knew how to play the game.
He tracked a dozen Herefords from
Tamworth out to Bourke
Using nothing more than instinct and a
passion for his work.

63

And he busted up a rustling ring that
spanned the eastern states,
Without the aid of partners, just a few
words from his mates.
But if there ever was a case that forged
his reputation,
The Homing Pigeon Hit spread his fame
across the nation.

The conman Kenny Carter was the master
of the scam,
For years it was his living, or in his words
bread and jam,
By day he sold his pigeons to
unsuspecting folk
And by night they'd all be home again – a
money-making joke.

So, with a bank of 50 pigeons which he
sold three times a week,
Ken was loving life, somewhere west of
Scrubby Creek.
The hideaway was secret but with Riley on
the trailThe boys back at the station knew
they'd soon have Ken in jail.

With a torch taped to his saddle shining
upwards from his horse
Riley rode non-stop for ninety miles to
track one pigeon's course.

He dismounted at the hideaway, tied up his
faithful mare,
Carter met him at the door, hands up in
the air.

He stood there looking sheepish, pondering
his fate,
Then Riley asked the question *'Aaaah, how
ya goin' mate?'*
'I thought at first,' the conman said *'that you
were young and green'*
*'But I've gotta hand it to ya, you're the best
I've ever seen.'*
Now there seemed no other option and
everyone conceded
To track down Mrs Johnston's chooks the
Roundup man was needed.
'I hear we've got a problem,' it was a voice
the crew all knew.
*'Mrs Johnston's chooks eh, well let's see what
we can do.'*

Now a lesser stock detective would've
headed for the scrub
But Riley's intuition took him straight
down to the pub.
His modus operandi, at first it
seemed unclear,
Then came the explanation, *'I just wouldn't
mind a beer'*.

He quietly quaffed a schooner as the boys
fed him the facts,
It was then that he decided on his method
of attack.
He rode to Mrs Johnston's while the others
drove behind
Wondering just what it was Riley hoped
to find.

He walked into the chookhouse, had a
look around,
*'Right, I'll take it all from here thanks boys,
you head back to town.'*
Now they don't know what he saw, Riley
wouldn't say,
He just jumped up on his horse and swiftly
rode away.

Forty minutes later he was at the
Kelly place
With Old Man Kelly standing there, broken
teeth and crooked face,
Riley walked towards him, leaned across
the gate,
Looked him up and down and said *'How ya
goin' mate?'*

And as he asked the question he noticed
near some trees
A single leghorn feather floating softly on
the breeze.
He looked long and hard at Kelly and said
'Now you just tell me straight
'Where you may have chanced to be last night
at half-past eight.'
'You see I've got the feeling you might be the
type of crook
'Low enough to rustle poor Mrs
Johnston's chooks.
'Now you don't have to do it but if you tell me
where they are
'I just might be convinced to put away this
iron bar.'

Old Kelly mumbled something, he couldn't
do much more,
Then pointed out a shaky arm towards a
grain-shed door.
Therein lay the missing birds which soon
were taken home
While Riley helped old Kelly pack his
toothbrush and his comb.

Mrs Johnston was delighted to have back her missing flock,
All her lovely leghorns and her little bantam cock.
She said to Roundup Riley *'I truly thank the Lord*
'And the only thing for me to do is offer you reward.'
Now Riley wasn't bashful so he thought he'd try his luck,
'I tell ya Mrs Johnston, I wouldn't mind the duck.'
Riley got his dinner and his reputation grew
But he never shared his secrets with the other boys in blue.

Just how he solved his cases was a mystery to all
But if you start out stealing stock, well, you're bound to get a call.
You'll see this bearded gentleman leaning on your gate,
He'll look you up and down and ask *'How ya goin' mate?'*

A PIG'S LAMENT

People say I'm ugly, people say I'm fat,
People say a lot of things a darn sight
worse than that.
They say I like to live in slop, they say
my hygiene's crook,
They say my life is total filth – but I tell
ya, they're mistook.

I may be just a pig to them who rolls in
mud and sludge
But who are they to criticise? Who are
they to judge?
If I'm given half a chance I'm really
very clean,
I don't throw rubbish in the creek or
breathe in nicotine.

I don't pump smoke into the air or
sewage to the sea,
There are a lot of things that I don't do
but still they pick on me.
Well, it's only fair I get the chance to
have a little dig,
You can keep your humans 'cause I'd
rather be A PIG!

THE FROGGYWOGS, THE LOGS & THE WAGGA WAGGA FOG

One day in Wagga Wagga the Froggywogs
got bogged
In their red rust-bucket truck that was
loaded up with logs,
They were flying through the fog when
they swerved to miss a dog
And now the Froggywogs were bogged in
the Wagga Wagga fog.

The logs bogged in the fog were for the
Buzztown Bees
They'd rung the Froggywogs and said
'We'd like some logs now, please,'
*'Our firewood's run out and it's minus
3 degrees!'*
Unless the Frogs un-bogged the logs the
Buzztown Bees would freeze!

Things were looking hopeless but the
Froggywogs struck luck,

Fearless Freddie Flying Fox and Dangerous
Dudley Duck
Were heading to Temora in the Shire
Fire-truck
And somehow through the fog they could
see the Frogs were stuck.

'*We'll get you out*,' yelled Fred, he had a lot
of brains,
'*All you have to do is hook up to this chain.*'
They quickly pulled them out just as it
began to rain
And pretty soon the Froggywogs were on
the road again.

The Buzztown Bees, they didn't freeze,
they finally got their logs
Thanks to Fearless Fred and Dudley and of
course the Froggywogs.
Who still laugh about the time when they
swerved to miss a dog
And bogged a load of logs in the Wagga
Wagga fog.

THROUGH THE EYES
OF BANJO

I have never battled drought on the
stations farther out,
Never turned my hand to droving when
there's little feed about,
I can't say I've danced a swag across a
lonely mountain pass
Nor sparred it with a squatter just to get
my sheep some grass,
I wouldn't make a stockman's stirrup so
it's prob'ly well disguised
That I've seen it all before — through
another poet's eyes.

I first learned to love this land through the
words penned by his hand,
First learned of legend characters like
Clancy and
The Man,
I Dead-Man-Creeked with Mulga Bill,
helped baptise young Magee
And the Geebung boys would never think
of playing without me.

I was there to cheer home Pardon, heard a
lovesick mother's cries,
Wept with raw emotion through another
poet's eyes.

I read of war and Federation and a
heartfelt obligation
To lend a guiding hand to the shaping of a
nation,
Fighting for what's right through the
power of the pen,
I only hope in the hereafter that The Banjo
rides again,
For his 'footprints in the lava' are the spark
that lit the fire
And that flame still burns today in another
poet's eyes.

GOING BACK TO SCHOOL

One of the cool things I get to do is poetry workshops at schools in rural NSW and Queensland. Robert Nowlan is the boss at Injune State School and he also coordinates my visits to some of the smaller schools in central Queensland (some with less than 10 students). Taking the kids' ideas and helping them to create limericks and poems is fantastic fun. Here is a selection from some of the schools I have visited.

FROM INJUNE
STATE SCHOOL

Fresha Voca Dos (aka Fresh Avocados)

We bought some mushrooms and
some pickles,
A loaf of bread, a bag of prickles,
A funny bunny on a dunny
And then when we ran out of money
We went out to my uncle's house,
Saw Donald Duck and Mini Mouse,
Both were playing piccolos
Eating fresha voca dos.
When it got dark, twinkle, twinkle,
The sky lit up with periwinkles.
Then we saw a flying sheep
And just before we went to sleep
We had to rub my uncle's bunions
While he ate a bowl of onions!
He stank so much we ran away
And when we got home on Saturday
The weather had turned really weird,
The dust and heat had disappeared.
Huge black clouds filled the sky,
The thunder boomed, the heaven's cried.
We all got drenched by Heaven's tears,
It hadn't rained for seven years.
It really was a magic day
And my uncle he got washed away.

MAD MICK SAVES CHRISTMAS

It was Christmas out at Injune and
really flamin' hot
Any hopes of snowing were well and
truly shot.
Frosty would've melted, Rudolph
would've fried
And in his big red suit poor old Santa
would've died.
So who would bring the presents to make
the children laugh again?
Because a Christmas without presents
would be really, really lame.
Then Bazza scratched his noggin and said
'I think we're all in luck,'
'Mad Mick, the emu shooter, just bought a
brand new truck.'
So Christmas Eve arrived, Mick turned up
at the pub,
He loaded up the presents and headed for
the scrub.
He was flying down the fire trail, talking to
his dog,
Took a corner way too quick and hit a mob
of hogs.

The truck was written off, Mick caught
six kangaroos,
Filled their pouches up with presents and
the roos began to cruise
Around the Injune countryside dropping
presents on the way
And all the kids were happy when they
woke on Christmas Day.

Now every Christmas out at Injune when
they gather for a beer
And talk about the heroes of the town
throughout the years,
The greatest of them all, you'll hear the
locals says
Was Mad Mick the Emu Shooter when he
played Santa for the day.

SCARY POEM

At the edge of town where the wild
wind blows
There stands a house where no one goes
Busted floorboards, windows broken,
Overgrown, doors half open
But people say that late at night
Inside there is an eerie light,
Crazy voices, evil laughter,
No chance of happily ever after.
The rumours go that long since past
A very evil spell was cast
By a witch, old and haggard,
Her nose was big, her clothes were ragged.
The spell she cast said all shall die
If they ever tell a lie
But now we're running out of time
We have to end this scary rhyme
Where will we go, what can we do
The rumour, well, it isn't true.
I made it up to write a poem,
Now it's time to all go home.

LIMERICKS

There was a young girl from Japan
Who danced on a red rubber band,
In a bit if bad luck
She got hit by a duck
Which just wasn't part of the plan.

There was a young boy from Peru
Who was paddling in his canoe
But his little red boat
Wasn't able to float
And he somehow got flushed down
the loo.

Santa flew into town
And with him came Krusty the Clown,
While Santa he blew
On a didgeridoo
Krusty was getting' on down.

FROM MITCHELL

The silly billygoat wore a really silly coat
And a stupid pair of purple underpants
But he got into a muddle when he stepped
into a puddle
And his pants got full of underwater ants.

A kitten who wore mittens went out and
chased a dog,
The dog hid in a log and got frightened by
a frog.
The dog chewed on a piece of bark and
very nearly choked,
The frog thought this was funny so he just
sat back and croaked.

FROM ARCADIA VALLEY

I'm Dreaming of A Wet Christmas

Dear Santa,
It's Christmas in the bush and the sun is
beating down
We have to buy some presents so we're
heading into town.
We all like toys and lollies but to ease a
lot of pain
The best present we could get would be
60mls of rain.
Rain to stop the fires, rain to drench
the earth
But you cannot buy the rain and we don't
know what it's worth
But it makes the farmers happy when
everything turns green
So if it's not a hassle, if it doesn't sound
too mean,
Let's forget about the presents, we don't
need toys this year,
Although Mum would like a holiday and
dad would like a beer,
All we really want is smiles when the
family gets together
So Santa could you bring us please some
wet and stormy weather.

FROM ST MARIA GORETTI PRIMARY SCHOOL, INGLEWOOD

(Written during an online session with the whole school)

Inglewood's got a great school,

At this school there aren't any fools,

The classrooms are clean,

The teachers are keen

And the students are all very cool.

I spoke to the students today,

It took a while to get underway,

We laughed and we rhymed,

Had a really good time

And they all had plenty to say.

I will see them in person for sure,

I can't wait to walk through the door,

It will give me a buzz

To say 'G'day, I'm Muz',

I just hope I don't fall on the floor.